She was a lovely lady in every way. She never expected to be Queen of England. When Edward the VIII gave up his birthright to marry a twice divorced American, Wally Simpson, it was a world shattering event. Changed the course of history - perhaps for the better because George, his brother, became a very good King of England with a very special woman as Queen, during the frightening years to come - World War II and beyond.

Their first child, Elizabeth, ultimately succeeded to the throne. She, like her dedicated parents, has served her country well, during many somber years for England.

Royal Family Library

The Queen Mother

CRESCENT – New York

Introduction

Affectionately known the world over as 'The Queen Mum', Elizabeth Angela Marguerite, youngest daughter of the fourteenth Earl and Countess of Strathmore, was born at St Paul's, Walden Bury in Hertfordshire on 4th August 1900. There were ten children in the family. Her younger brother David was almost like a twin.

Elizabeth was christened at Glamis Castle in Scotland, the family's stronghold since the fourteenth century, and spent much of her childhood there. This old, turreted castle came to her family when Princess Joan, daughter of King Robert II, married Sir John Lyon, Keeper of the Privy Seal, from whom the Queen Mother is directly descended. It is a strange, even forbidding place filled with an atmosphere of magic and mystery. Among the royal heirlooms is a watch said to have been left behind by Bonnie Prince Charlie.

Her childhood was typical of Edwardian days. She had ponies to ride (her favourite was one named Bobs) and dogs to play with, and she enjoyed a busy social life. In her fourteenth year the First World War began and life was suddenly very different for Elizabeth. Her brothers joined the army. Fergus was killed in 1915 at the Battle of Loos, and Michael was taken prisoner. Elizabeth joined her mother and sisters at Glamis Castle which had been turned into a convalescent home for wounded soldiers. Soon, the young girl was caught up in a whirl of nursing, helping by writing letters and shopping and entertaining the men by playing the piano. She treated the men as honoured guests in her mother's home.

Following the custom of those days, she had been educated privately and her work with the wounded was her first contact with 'ordinary' people. One night the castle caught fire and it was her quick thinking, when she helped to quench the flames, which saved her home before the arrival of the fire brigade.

After the war she came to London, and took her place in the Society of the Twenties. She was a keen Girl Guide and met the Princess Royal who was very interested in the Movement. Later she was bridesmaid at the Royal marriage of the Princess to Lord Lascelles. She often visited Buckingham Palace where King George V and Queen Mary were enchanted by her. Here she met the young Duke of York who had served in the Royal Navy at the Battle of Jutland. The friendship strengthened and, in 1923, they became engaged with the consent of the King and Queen. The wedding took place at Westminster Abbey on 26th April 1923, with the Prince of Wales as groomsman and eight bridesmaids in attendance. On the morning of the wedding, King George V invested his son with the Order of the Thistle as a gesture to honour his Scottish daughter-in-law. The Duke wore the honour at the ceremony. A Scottish piper played for Elizabeth as she walked to the altar and on her way she left her bouquet on the tomb of the Unknown Warrior and was married without flowers in her hand.

So, a new and busy life began. At first, the Duke and Duchess of York were able to live quietly, performing some public functions. Among their homes was White Lodge in Richmond Park which still belongs to the Queen Mother. Their first child, Elizabeth, was born at her parents' home in Bruton Street, London. Shortly afterwards, the Duke and Duchess went on a six months tour of New Zealand and the child was left with Queen Mary.

Their second child, Princess Margaret, was born at Glamis Castle in Scotland in 1930. By then her parents had a London home at 145 Piccadilly. In 1935, the country celebrated the Silver Jubilee of King George V and Queen Mary, but the following year was a sad one because King George V died and Edward VIII abdicated. The unthinkable had happened. There was no alternative but for the Duke to become King George VI, and together with the Queen shouldered the heavy burdens of royalty.

In May 1937, King George VI and Queen Elizabeth were crowned at Westminster Abbey, and in June that year she was made a Lady of the Order of the Garter in recognition of her support for the King. In 1938, they paid a state visit to France, the first of a reigning monarch since 1914, and in 1939 their tour of Canada and the United States was an undoubted success. The King, the first member of the Royal Family to fly an aeroplane himself, met President Roosevelt who was the first American President to fly.

In September 1939 the Second World War was declared. The Queen visited people in all parts of the country, sharing their sorrows and hopes and, above all, encouraging them. Her children lived at Windsor while she and the King stayed at Buckingham Palace throughout. When the Palace was bombed, she is said to have remarked that she could look the East Enders in the face now that she had shared their sufferings. The Queen played a vital role particularly with the Women's Services, and is said to have disapproved of the first Wren hat; it was promptly changed! When the Women's Land Army was formed in 1939 she became Patron. Remembering her days in the First World War she quickly organized knitting and sewing parties at Buckingham Palace with the Red Cross, and her visits to hundreds of hospitals and factories brought comfort to many. In 1939, the Queen broadcast a personal message of hope and encouragement to the women of the empire.

After the war there was the Royal tour of South Africa, followed by the excitement of Princess Elizabeth's wedding, and the birth of Prince Charles and Princess Anne. Then came the sad and sudden death of King George VI in 1952. The Queen was now the Queen Mother and had a new role to play in the future of her country.

Early Life

The Queen Mother, born into a happy family life in Scotland, possesses the rare gift of making the people she meets feel important. This has been borne out in the very real love she has attracted from the members of her family, as well as the general public. She proved herself a courageous woman, and an invaluable support to her husband when he was called upon to become King of England on the abdication of his brother in 1936. Throughout his reign, Queen Elizabeth was always his side to help, love and cherish the shy young Prince who had won her heart as a young woman.

During the war her home was bombed, and she shared it with the many foreign monarchs seeking sanctuary in England when their own countries were invaded. She played hostess to King Haakon of Norway, Queen Wilhel-mina of the Netherlands, Prince Bernhardt and her daughter Princess Juliana. Their daughter had not been christened, so she was baptised in the Chapel at Buckingham Palace, shortly before it was destroyed by enemy bombs. The Palace was bombed nine times and Cecil Beaton made a pictorial record of the damage.

In peacetime, the Queen's anxiety over her husband's health increased, although she had the great joy of her daughter's wedding, followed by the celebrations for her own Silver Wedding in St Paul's Cathedral in 1948. This was the same year as her first grandchild, Prince Charles, was born. In 1951, she and the King toured the Festival of Britain on the South Bank, but the following year George VI died and the Queen was a widow, her daughter a Queen.

Opposite *Glamis Castle in Scotland, where the Queen Mother spent most of her childhood.*

Above *The Queen Mother at a Buckingham Palace garden party for repatriated prisoners of war. Here, she is talking to allied soldiers of the Second World War.*

Right *An informal study of the King and Queen at Buckingham Palace.*

Left *Lady Elizabeth Angela Marguerite Bowes-Lyon, daughter of the Earl and Countess of Strathmore, pictured standing next to her mother and eight of her nine brothers and sisters, of whom she is the second youngest. The picture was taken at St Paul's, Walden Bury where she was born and spent much of her childhood.*

Below *The Queen Mother as a child of seven, wearing a fringe which she kept until after her marriage.*

Above left *A formal wedding day picture after their marriage at Westminster Abbey on 26th April 1923.*

Above right *The newly-married Duke and Duchess of York on their honeymoon at Bookham. They are seen leaving church after the morning service on 29th April 1923, three days after their marriage.*

Above *A delightful study of the Duchess of York taken in 1926, with her daughter Elizabeth.*

Left *A group photograph taken after the christening of Princess Elizabeth, their eldest child, in May 1926. It shows King George V and Queen Mary, the Duke and Duchess of York, The Duke of Connaught, Princess Mary and the mother's parents, the Earl and Countess of Strathmore.*

Above *During the royal tour of 1927, the Duke and Duchess on a trip down Brisbane river on the yacht* Juanita.

Left *A wet homecoming for the Duke and Duchess. The Duchess is seen holding up the infant Princess Elizabeth on the balcony of Buckingham Palace on 27th June 1927.*

Opposite above right *After their Coronation on 12th May 1937, King George VI and Queen Elizabeth acknowledge the cheers of the crowds from the balcony of Buckingham Palace.*

Opposite *King George VI and Queen Elizabeth, with their daughters, Princess Elizabeth and Princess Margaret, taken in Buckingham Palace in 1939. A family corgi has joined them.*

Opposite centre right *The King and Queen enjoy the traditional New York welcome when they drive down West Side Highway on 10th June 1939 on their way to the New York World Fair.*

Opposite below right *During the Second World War, the Queen received a great reception at Stepney when she toured the blitzed East End of London.*

Left *King George VI and Queen Elizabeth taken at Buckingham Palace in April 1948, on the occasion of their Silver Wedding.*
Below left *Her Majesty holding her first grandchild, Prince Charles, after his christening at Buckingham Palace in 1948.*
Below *The Queen Mother in 1954 on the terrace of Royal Lodge, Windsor, with Prince Charles and Princess Anne.*
Opposite above left *The Queen Mother in Kenya at the foot of the jungle hotel, Treetops, in the Aberdare Forest.*
Opposite centre left *The Queen Mother meeting a group of Masai women at Narok in Kenya, accompanied by the Governor, Sir Evelyn Baring.*
Opposite below left *The Queen Mother with Prince Charles and Princess Anne on a shopping expedition near Balmoral.*
Opposite above right *On 31st October 1972, in celebration of the Royal Silver Wedding, the family took part in the annual Ghillies' Ball at Balmoral.*
Opposite centre right *Celebrating St Patrick's Day with the Irish Guards at Windsor.*
Opposite below right *A seventy-fifth birthday portrait with Princes Charles and Andrew.*

Left *A wartime photograph of the King and Queen with their children at Buckingham Palace in 1942.*
Below *Pictured in 1947, the King and Queen with their daughters and Prince Philip.*

Above *Queen Elizabeth on the Royal couple's visit to the Festival of Britain site on the South Bank in 1951.*
Right *The body of King George VI lying in state in Westminster Hall in 1952, prior to his funeral. The coffin is draped with the Royal Standard, and on top are the Imperial Crown and the Queen Mother's wreath.*

Life in Public

After the death of King George VI in 1952, the Queen Mother might have been expected to retire from public life, but she immediately assumed the role of mother rather than wife, helping her daughter over the first, difficult years of monarchy. A veritable tower of strength, she once again dedicated herself to the unfailing service of others, without thought for herself.

Owing to the King's increasing illness in 1951, she was the first Queen Dowager to be appointed a Counsellor of State. She still deputizes for her daughter when the Queen is away on official duties.

The Queen Mother has a wide range of interests and is Patron or President of over three hundred organizations including the Royal Academy of Music, Girl Guides, Women's Section of the Royal British Legion, WRVS, YWCA and Women's Services. She is Chancellor of a number of Universities in England and overseas, was made Master of the Bench of the Middle Temple in 1944, and in 1958 was the first member of the Royal family to fly around the world. She has made many tours over the years and is a welcome visitor at home and abroad. It has been said that she performs every duty as if it were for the first time, and has an amazing love of life and people. She is known for her knowledge of flowers and gardens, and never misses the Annual Chelsea Flower Show in the grounds of the Royal Hospital in May of each year.

Whatever the occasion, whether it be the pageantry of the Garter Ceremony at Windsor, Royal Ascot, the Jubilee Celebrations or a simple ceremony at a veterans' home or hospital, the Queen Mother adds grace and charm by her presence.

A singular honour conferred on her in 1979 was her appointment as the first woman Warden of the Cinque Ports at Dover Castle on 1st August.

Ceremonies

Opposite *The Queen Mother is welcomed on her arrival in Uganda in 1954. Here she is inspecting a guard of honour in the sunshine.*
Left *On a visit to Sydney, Australia, the Queen Mother inspects members of the Women's Services.*
Below *A scholastic occasion when the Queen Mother conferred degrees at Berry University in Rhodesia.*

Left *Queen Elizabeth, the Queen Mother, was made a Lady of the Order of the Garter in 1936. She takes part in the Annual Ceremony at St George's Chapel, Windsor. She is also a Lady of the Order of the Thistle.*
Below *In 1972, the Queen Mother accompanied the Emperor of Ethiopia, Haile Selassie, to the Garter Ceremony. Here they are making their way past the knights and gentleman-at-arms lining their route.*

Above *Accompanied by Prince Charles, the Queen Mother is driven away after the Garter Ceremony.*
Left *The Queen Mother carrying out an inspection of a guard of honour. She is Colonel-in-Chief of a number of regiments.*

17

Opposite *The Queen conferring the Honorary Degree of Doctor of Music on her mother at the Royal College of Music in December 1973.*
Left *With her younger daughter, Princess Margaret, riding in an open carriage to the Guildhall for a luncheon to celebrate the Queen's Silver Wedding in November 1972.*
Below *The Queen Mother riding with Princess Anne in an open landau to watch the annual Trooping the Colour at Horse Guards Parade on 12th June 1976.*

Opposite *With her grandsons, Prince Andrew, Prince Edward and Prince Charles in a bearskin, the Queen Mother rides through the streets of London after the Queen's Silver Jubilee Thanksgiving Service at St Paul's Cathedral on 7th June 1977.*
Below *On the balcony of Buckingham Palace after the Jubilee Service, the Queen Mother stands with the rest of the Royal Family to acknowledge the cheers of the thousands of people who had gathered at the Palace.*

Above *On her way to her installation as the first lady and member of the Royal Family to be made Warden of the Cinque Ports on 1st August 1979.*
Left *The Queen Mother, always ready to speak to a child, stops to talk to a small girl after the official ceremonies at Dover Castle.*
Opposite *The grey splendour of Dover Castle makes a marvellous backcloth as the Queen Mother's coach procession wends its way after her installation as Warden of the Cinque Ports. This office dates back to the days of William the Conqueror; her immediate predecessors in office have included Sir Winston Churchill and Sir Robert Menzies.*

Below *Taken to mark her seventy-fifth birthday in August 1975, the Queen Mother is wearing a dress of white chiffon embroidered with patterns of gold beads, with a diamond* *tiara, diamond drop earrings, diamond bracelet and diamond and pearl necklace. She is also wearing the Sash of the Order of the Garter and Star with Family Orders mounted in diamonds.*

Opposite *A charming close-up of the Queen Mother taken on the same occasion – her seventy-fifth birthday.*

General

Left *The Queen Mother enjoying the sunshine at a country fair.*
Below *The Queen Mother is the friend of all animals. Here she has a word of admiration for a donkey at the fair.*
Opposite above *A great lover of flowers and gardens, the Queen Mother inspects the exhibits at the 1963 Sandringham Flower Show.*
Opposite below *The Royal visitor pausing to admire a particularly fine display of roses at the 1963 Sandringham Flower Show.*

Opposite above *The Queen Mother smiles as she receives a bouquet at the Braemar Games in Scotland. The Queen is at her side.*

Opposite below *With Princess Margaret in the Royal Drive at Ascot, cheered by the watching crowds.*

Right *The Queen Mother arriving at Cheltenham station for the start of the National Hunt Festival in March 1967.*

Below *A day on 'the flat' – the Queen Mother at the 1967 Derby at Epsom.*

Below right *The Queen Mother at the Derby on 1st June 1977 with the Duke and Duchess of Kent. Unfortunately, her daughter's horse did not win the Jubilee Derby!*

Above *With Princess Josephine
Charlotte, Grand Duchess of
Luxembourg, in an open
carriage for the traditional
Royal drive at Royal Ascot in
June 1975.*
Left *The Queen Mother talking
knowledgeably in the unsaddling
enclosure at Royal Ascot.*
Opposite *Wearing one of her
particularly pretty outfits, at
Royal Ascot with her daughter.*

Opposite *A charming, informal study of the Queen Mother in her garden, before going to an official function.*

Below *The Queen Mother arrives at a function wearing an attractive turquoise velvet outfit, and a charming smile.*

Below *The Queen Mother leaving St Paul's Cathedral after attending a Memorial Service for President Eisenhower in April 1969.*

Opposite *The Queen Mother opening the Gardening Centre at Syon House in Middlesex on 10th June 1968.*

Below *With flowers forming her favourite background, the Queen Mother standing in the grounds of Royal Lodge, Windsor, on the occasion of her seventieth birthday.*

Opposite *The Queen Mother attending an official engagement. She arrived by helicopter. The Royal Family often use this method of transport for convenience and speed.*

Top *Planting a tree to commemorate her visit to the Queen Elizabeth Foundation for the Disabled at Leatherhead in July 1970.*

Above *During her annual New Year visit to Sandringham, the Queen Mother at the Whitefriars Church of England School at King's Lynn in January 1971. She is seen here admiring the work of the children.*

Opposite *At a charity performance, the Queen Mother pauses to speak to the well-known entertainer, Danny La Rue, while comedian Ken Dodd looks on.*

Left *Unveiling a plaque to commemorate the opening of the New Croydon YMCA in April 1974.*
Below *Prior to the opening of the New Croydon YMCA, the Queen Mother inspects a guard of honour.*

Above *Admiring a bouquet of roses presented to her after she had opened the extension to Kingswood Grange Veterans' Home near Reigate in Surrey in July 1974.*
Left *The Queen Mother talking to one of the residents at Kingswood Grange.*

Opposite *The Queen Mother after opening Denman College.*
Right *The Queen Mother seen leaving HMS Bronington after a visit to her grandson, Prince Charles, who was captain of the mine-hunter at the time. Other members of the Royal party are seen in the background. Judging from her poppy and black coat, the visit must have taken place in November.*
Below *The Queen, her mother, Prince Philip, Prince Charles and Princess Margaret entertain world leaders who came to London for a two-day Downing Street summit in May 1977. They are seen here in the Blue Drawing Room at Buckingham Palace.*

Opposite *The Queen Mother, dressed in an attractive pink outfit, photographed before attending an official engagement.*
Right *The Queen Mother photographed on her seventy-fifth birthday – 4th August 1975. She is wearing one of her famous feathery hats.*
Below *An outdoor person, the Queen Mother enjoys walking in her gardens in the sunshine. This is one of a series of birthday portrait photographs taken on 4th August 1970.*

Private Life

The Queen Mother is a very private lady and is happiest with her family, either relaxing in Scotland, Windsor, Sandringham, which holds many memories for her, or in London where her grandchildren are constant visitors.

A countrywoman at heart, she always enjoys being outdoors. As Duchess of York, she introduced the famous corgis into the Royal Household, and is rarely seen without one on her walks. She often watches her grand-daughter competing at equestrian events such as Badminton, or her own steeplechasers taking part in the National Hunt Festival at Cheltenham or in the Grand National. Although she enjoys all forms of racing, she has concentrated her considerable knowledge of horses on 'chasers while the Queen breeds and races horses for the 'flat'. She is a good sport and when her horse, Devon Loch, was narrowly beaten in the closing seconds of the 1956 Grand National, her immediate concern was for the jockey and his feelings.

She always spends part of the summer in her native Scotland where she has two homes – Birkhall on the Balmoral estate, and the Castle of Mey on the shores of Caithness. While staying with a friend in the area soon after the King's death, she saw the sixteenth century Barrogill Castle, once home of the Earls of Caithness. It had fallen into disrepair, but she decided to buy and restore it, renaming it the Castle of Mey. Now, thanks to her efforts, the gardens are ablaze with the colours of beautiful flowers, and the shoreline is a paradise for birds which she can watch from the windows.

It can be said without contradiction that the Queen Mother, with her charm and energy, transforms the lives of people with whom she is in contact and revitalizes the houses she lives in, be they old castles in Scotland or houses in London and Windsor. She is the living witness of one who, in the words of Kipling, can 'walk with kings – nor lose the common touch'.

Left Accompanied by two of her favourite corgi dogs, the Queen Mother waves as she prepares to board a train.
Opposite Clarence House in the Mall, the Queen Mother's London home, is immediately opposite the historic old Palace of St James. From its windows, it is possible to witness the traditional proclamation ceremony in Friary Court when a new sovereign ascends the throne. It was designed by John Nash and originally built for the Duke of Clarence, who became William IV. It later became the home of the Duke of Connaught, seventh child of Queen Victoria, but it fell into disrepair when he was appointed Governor-General of Canada in 1911. The Red Cross used part of it as offices in the Second World War when it was bombed. In 1947, when the Queen and Prince Philip made it their home, it had no bathrooms, no electricity and poor gas lighting. It was completely renovated and in 1949 the Royal couple moved in. They lived there for three years and Princess Anne was born there in 1950. It was in this house that the first official condolences were offered to the Queen on the death of her father, and members of the government had their first audiences with her. The Queen and Prince Philip later moved into Buckingham Palace and the Queen Mother took up residence at Clarence House.

Below *An informal portrait of the Queen Mother in the garden on her seventieth birthday with three of her grandchildren and two of her dogs.*

Opposite *A happy occasion! Princess Anne, grand-daughter of the Queen Mother, and her husband Captain Mark Phillips leaving Westminster Abbey after their wedding on 14th*

November 1973. The Royal Family, in the background, are watching their departure. The wedding day happened to be the birthday of Prince Charles.

This happy group photograph shows the Royal family and friends after the wedding of Lord Patrick Lichfield (the well-known Society photographer) to Lady Leonora Grosvenor, daughter of the Duke of Westminster in 1975. It was called 'The Wedding of the Year'. The Queen Mother is related to the bridegroom, through her niece, Anne Bowes-Lyon, who married Lord Lichfield's father.

Below *A charming study of the Queen Mother taken to mark her seventieth birthday in August 1970. This picture was taken at Royal Lodge, Windsor.*

Opposite *The Queen Mother and other members of the Royal family attend the wedding of the Duke of Gloucester and the Danish-born Birgitte van Deurs in July 1972.*

Overleaf *A family group at Windsor for the Royal Silver Wedding in 1972. The picture was taken by Lord Patrick Lichfield.*

53

Left *The Royal family at the Badminton Horse Trials. They watch intently as the horses are paraded on the Sunday morning for the veterinary inspection, before the final phase of the Three-Day Event – show-jumping.*
Below left *The Queen Mother at Badminton. Perhaps she is following her grand-daughter's progress round the course?*
Below right *The Queen Mother, well-protected against the weather, at the Badminton Horse Trials.*
Opposite *The Queen and Queen Mother in informal dress stand in the wooded surroundings of Badminton House enjoying the spectacle of the Three-Day Event.*

Above *With field-glasses to her eyes, the Queen Mother stands on a wagon with Prince Edward and the Duke of Beaufort to watch the Badminton Horse Trials.*

Right *Accompanied by Prince Andrew, another keen spectator, the Queen Mother watches the thrills and excitement of the Trials.*

Opposite *The Queen Mother with a kilted Prince Charles at the Braemar Games in Scotland.*

Right *A smiling Queen Mother with the Duchess of Kent.*
Below *The Queen Mother at Badminton with Princess Alexandra and the Hon Angus Ogilvy, and their son, the Hon James Ogilvy.*
Opposite *The Queen, Queen Mother and Princess Anne after the christening of her son, Peter Mark, who was born on the 15th November 1977. His birthday is one day after his mother's wedding anniversary and the birthday of Prince Charles. Peter Phillips is the Queen Mother's first great-grandson.*

Opposite *A formal portrait of
the Queen Mother with one of
her corgis at Clarence House.*
Above *The Queen Mother at
Clarence House acknowledging
the cheers of the crowd outside,
on the occasion of her seventy-
eighth birthday.*
Right *The Queen Mother
pictured during the state funeral
service for Lord Louis
Mountbatten, a dearly loved
member of the family. The
service took place at
Westminster Abbey on
Wednesday, 5th September
1979, and the burial was at
Romsey Abbey.*

A happy scene at Clarence House. The Queen Mother, celebrating her seventy-ninth birthday, smiles at the crowds of well-wishers who are reluctant to see her go inside. She is accompanied by some of her grandchildren – Prince Edward, and the son and daughter of Princess Margaret, Viscount Linley and Lady Sarah Armstrong-Jones. Public affection for the Queen Mother never diminishes, and every year on her birthday, which she always spends in London, crowds gather from early in the day. English and tourists alike, they come to greet a beloved Queen Mother.

Acknowledgements

The publishers would like to thank the following for their help in supplying photographs for this book.

All photographs are by courtesy of Camera Press Limited except those listed below:

The Associated Press: Page 9 (centre right)

Fox Photos Limited: Page 5 (bottom), page 12 (top), page 13, page 18, page 35, page 38 (top and bottom), page 48.

Keystone Press Agency Limited: Pages 22–23, page 43 (top).

Popperfoto: Page 6 (top), page 7 (top right and bottom), page 8, page 9 (top), page 10 (bottom right), page 12 (bottom).

The Press Association Limited: Page 43 (bottom), page 49.

First English edition published 1980 by
Intercontinental Book Productions, Berkshire House,
Queen Street, Maidenhead, Berkshire, England
Copyright © MCMLXXX by Intercontinental Book Productions
All rights reserved
This edition is published by Crescent Books, a division of Crown
Publishers, Inc, by arrangement with Intercontinental Book
Productions
A B C D E F G H
Printed in Hong Kong

Library of Congress Cataloging in Publication Data

Leete-Hodge, Lornie.
  The Queen Mother.

  1. Elizabeth, Consort of George VI, 1900–
– Iconography. 2. Great Britain – Queens – Iconography.
I. Title.
DA585.A2L4   1980   941.084′092′4 [B]   79-25211
ISBN 0-517-30812-6